UNDERSTANDING GRIEF

Martina E. Faulkner MSW

INSPIREBYTES OMNI MEDIA

This publication is published and distributed worldwide in the English language in the following formats:

ISBN Paperback: 978-1-953445-75-9
ISBN E-Book: 978-1-953445-76-6

This book was printed in a manner that minimizes its impact on the planet and the environment. Learn more at: www.inspirebytes.com/why-we-publish-differently/

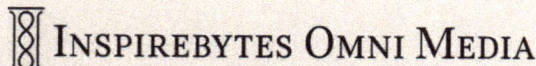 INSPIREBYTES OMNI MEDIA

Inspirebytes Omni Media LLC
PO Box 988
Wilmette, IL 60091

For more information, please visit www.inspirebytes.com
Graphics and photos: Canva Design Pro

For everyone who has experienced loss and
searched for answers to questions they didn't know how to ask...

I hope this helps.

Contents

"The bird is gone, and in what meadow does it now sing?"

– Philip K. Dick –

Introduction

Grief is a topic that everyone will need to address at some point in their lives. It's a common experience that is experienced individually. It both invites us into a new way of understanding life, while simultaneously thrusting us into changes we often don't want. It is the "push-me/pull-you" of all emotions, both causing despair in the midst of loss, while also reminding us of the depth of love or the promise of hope.

When we truly understand grief for what it is, life can somehow become easier, even though it was hardship that brought us to this point. In that way, grief is a great teacher, and just like all teachers, it brings us lessons we may feel unprepared to learn... or are unwilling to learn.

However, when we allow ourselves to pause and become open to grief, we can find a peace that we previously didn't think possible. To understand this better, we have to break it down and truly get to the heart of what it is, what it does, and how we can move through it. This is the irony of grief: It is both a torment and a blessing.

What is Grief?

"If there ever comes a day where we can't be together, keep me in your heart. I'll stay there forever."

— A.A. Milne, Winnie the Pooh —

In its simplest explanation, grief is all of the unexpressed love or hope we have for someone or something we've lost. This is why it's overwhelming at times and why we can feel "overtaken by grief."

Think of it like this:

You have a reservoir of love and hope inside you that you get to share over time. As you meet people with whom you want to share your love, you connect a hose to them and start to let your love flow into them, just as their love flows back to you from their reservoir.

Over the course of your life, your reservoir continually flows to people or situations in this way through small or steady doses. This allows you to experience love and hope in an ongoing way for years and years.

When we lose someone or something, the whole system suddenly changes and the steady flow still has to go somewhere but it can't.

So it backs up and becomes an enormous pond of all the unexpressed things we didn't get to share or do. Like a garden hose that can't be turned off but no longer has a receptacle to fill, it just keeps flowing—only now it's collecting inside you.

This is especially true when the loss occurs out of our expected order of things, chronologically, such as losing a child or a sibling at a young age. In those cases, the grief can feel insurmountable because there was so much love stored up with the expectation that we would have decades to share it.

The grief we carry from loss is often a form of unexpressed emotions, such as love. Therefore, the depth of grief is often experienced in direct proportion to the depth of the lost opportunity. For example, the more you loved someone, the more grief you may experience when they are gone since it feels like there's nowhere for your deep love to go.

Similarly, the more unexpected the loss, the deeper the resulting pain can be as it may match the intensity of the loss itself.

"The risk of love is loss, and the price of loss is grief —
But the pain of grief is only a shadow when
compared with the pain of never risking love."
— Hilary Stanton Zunin —

To further the issue, when this pool of unexpressed emotions is denied, ignored, or stuffed away, it can fester as it continues to grow. It needs an outlet. As such, all grief—regardless of its cause—requires some measure of mourning.

Whether the loss is from something tangible (like death) or less-tangible (like loss of a promotion or opportunity), you need to mourn in order to find healing and peace. The mourning process is what allows you to shift into a new perspective. It's the time in between that bridges reality and acceptance, ultimately creating a new reality.

To grieve without some sort of mourning is to remain in denial, which leaves the grief in an unresolved state and can prolong the experience. Over time, this can create more problems (such as a victim identity, for example) which undermines any potential for future happiness. Though mourning can hurt and means you have to acknowledge the loss and feel the grief, it's the healthiest way to move forward.

"To weep is to make less the depth of grief."

– William Shakespeare –

> *"The song is ended, but the melody lingers on."*
>
> — Irving Berlin —

Now that we know what grief is, we need to gain a better understanding of loss. What is loss, really? More importantly, why do we need to understand loss if we are to understand grief? Firstly, it's worth noting that you don't have to actually lose something to feel loss. Loss comes in many different shapes and sizes, but all loss triggers some form or expression of grief.

Typically, when talking about grief, the immediate assumption is that there has been a death. It's most closely associated with that type of loss, and it's where grief is discussed most often. However, loss of any kind can trigger grief. Therefore, it's important to know what loss truly means. To begin with, there are three distinct types of loss:

Physical loss —•— Emotional loss —•— Physical and emotional loss

Physical Loss

This is possibly the simplest form of loss and it usually involves an object of some sort. For example, a major car accident in which your car was totaled beyond repair could trigger a sense of physical loss, just like the loss of a wedding ring in the sand on a beach holiday. Though it's about an emotional attachment in some way, this kind of loss actually requires an object. This is true whether it's a favorite piece of jewelry or, in a worst case scenario, the loss of a home to a fire.

> *"Your memory feels like home to me. So whenever my mind wanders, it always finds its way back to you."*
>
> — Ranata Suzuki —

In these cases, the loss that is experienced is one that triggers a sadness for the memories the object contained or the expectation of the memories yet to be created. The loss is tangible and experienced in real time. It may also have lingering effects for a while, even as the item is replaced.

Emotional Loss

Different to physical loss, emotional loss implies an absence of a physical object. This means that this type of loss is more closely related to loss of opportunity or perception. For example, if you have been planning on a promotion at work and someone else is promoted instead, this is a perceived loss. The loss is experienced entirely emotionally because it's rooted in thought and expectation. In other words, the loss is related to something that was in your mind, instead of in your environment.

More often than not, emotional loss is likened to discouragement or disempowerment, such as loss of personal agency. These are both symptoms of feeling like something has gone from you or been taken from you—something you had previously experienced in your mind or hoped for. For example, not getting into your first choice of university can be an emotional loss.

The hope you once experienced in your thoughts falls away upon receipt of a rejection letter and in its place, grief shows up as a result of the perceived loss. Emotional loss, though less tangible than physical loss, can be deeply unsettling, at least for a little while.

Physical and Emotional Loss

This is, perhaps, the most commonly understood category of loss, because we can liken it to the greater majority of situations in our life. This is the type of loss that comes from death, divorce, major change, disease or illness, financial difficulties, and so much more.

This is the loss that most of us will experience at least once in our lives, if not more. It is also the loss that requires more patience and understanding when dealing with grief, because it's the type of loss that can result in grief that lasts for the remainder of our lives.

However, even though physical and emotional loss is the most common type, it can sometimes be the least accepted and understood. This means that it has the potential to be the least respected. Why? Because it can often trigger issues with comparative loss, which is a minefield, at best.

What is Comparative Loss?

Comparative loss is the mechanism by which we try to create a hierarchy for the experience of loss—instead of accepting that everyone's experience is valid and unique. This is a recipe for broken relationships as well as chronic disappointment, frustration, and ultimately, resentment.

The bottom line is that there is no way to accurately compare loss. There is no scale to weigh loss, because it is entirely individual. Nobody's life experiences are exactly the same as somebody else's.

Therefore, nobody can truly know what someone is experiencing—whether it's the loss of a loved one through death or the loss of a loved one through divorce, for example. To try to compare and equate loss is to set yourself up for more hurt and damaged relationships.

Placing a value on loss is to not understand it at its core: Loss is both unique and universal. Everyone experiences loss, and everyone that experiences loss does so differently. To suggest that there is a "better" or "worse" experience of loss is to disrespect the person who is grieving.

In short, it's best not to compare loss, as it rarely leads to anything positive, including healing. The warning here is to refrain from comparing and equating loss. Instead, the focus should be on understanding that loss is difficult and deeply personal and everyone needs time to mourn in their own way.

Once comparison is off the table, the one simple truth to understanding loss —and therefore understanding grief— is that everyone can relate to what it is. Though they may not know the nuanced details of the loss someone else is personally experiencing, everyone can understand what it feels like to go through loss. It is a human condition that very few people (if any) escape during their lifetime.

This commonality is what opens the door to understanding grief, and, more importantly, understanding how to heal.

"The friend who can be silent with us in a moment of despair or confusion, who can stay with us in an hour of grief and bereavement, who can tolerate not knowing… not healing, not curing… that is a friend who cares."

– Henri Nouwen –

How Long Do We Experience Grief?

"No matter how long it's been, there are times when it suddenly becomes harder to breathe."
— Anonymous —

When does grief end? Or does it end? These are questions most people ask when in the midst of grief, especially when relief feels out of reach. Once we understand that the essence of grief is tied to love, the duration of grief becomes entirely variable.

For some, the grief may last until they, themselves, take their last breath. For others, though the grief always remains, it can diminish in its intensity over the course of a lifetime. The grief doesn't go away; it just changes in proportion to the life you are living, the life you are adding to every day.

There is no one answer for how long grief can last, though some have suggested that there are formulas for it.

What's most important to remember is that the measure of grief will always reside in understanding its relationship to love, which can get more complicated when love is clouded by other emotions; the grief might be more drawn out or cut short.

Therefore, the best answer to the question "How long do we experience grief?" is actually: For as long as you need—or, perhaps, for as long as you want. In both instances, it takes as long as it takes, and there is no singular timeframe for grieving. There may be prescribed periods of mourning, depending on religion and culture, but grief is not the same as mourning, and how long grief lasts will always be unique to the individual.

"Sometimes, only one person is missing, and the whole world seems depopulated."
– Alphonse de Lamartine –

Understanding Mourning

Throughout history, different religious and cultural beliefs have mandated different practices for mourning. How you choose to mourn will be up to you and your specific situation. The variety of options can range significantly based on country, religion, and nationality, to name a few. From ceremonies and offerings, to the specific clothing worn or number of days required to appropriately mourn the loss of someone, mourning is a very personal endeavor. What's common among all these traditions is that mourning is inextricably linked to death.

> *"We all want to do something to mitigate the pain of loss or to turn grief into something positive, to find a silver lining in the clouds. But I believe there is real value in just standing there, being still, being sad."*
> *— John Green —*

Mourning in Relation to Death

In Western cultures, death is often not included in the discussion of life. It somehow seems counter-intuitive to talk about death when focusing on life, but nothing could be further from the truth. Death is part of the life cycle. Nobody escapes it, and it's completely natural. To try and tuck it away in a corner out of sight is to deny its existence.

Unfortunately, the taboo nature of discussing death contributes to the difficulty we have around truly understanding grief. Furthermore, alongside the desire to keep death out of the conversation, mourning is sometimes also sidelined. It can seem like there is shame around mourning, specifically when discussing the why, when, where, and how long we do it.

By keeping mourning and death at arms' length, we can unnaturally prolong the experience of grief. Though there is no prescribed amount of time to grieve, there is one certainty: Attempting to ignore grief or stuff it down will most certainly extend its duration.

Mourning in Relation to Loss

Since mourning is a part of the process of healing during grief, mourning also has to occur when there has been loss that isn't from somebody dying. Examples of this kind of loss can include:

- Losing something tangible (loss of a home to a fire)

- Losing a relationship (family, friends, romantic)

- Losing an opportunity (promotion, acceptance, etc.)

- Losing something previously relied on (the quality of a relationship)

All of these losses will require some acknowledgment of the grief so that you can appropriately mourn. Mourning these changes in your life in some way can help you accept them and move forward.

"Absence is a house so vast that inside you will pass through its walls and hang pictures on the air."

— Pablo Neruda —

Grieving as a Ratio and a Rhythm

The Ratio of Grief

There's one aspect about the duration of grief that seems to be consistent across all types and causes, which is that there is always a ratio involved. As long as you allow yourself to experience it, the grief will inevitably shrink in comparison to the rest of your life, if given the time. Time, in this instance, is the variable that makes it more tolerable. It's not that the grief is actually less, but the ratio of grief to the rest of your life changes over time. As your life continues, and your love for other things grows, the grief feels smaller and less consuming. It's a ratio, not a fixed percentage.

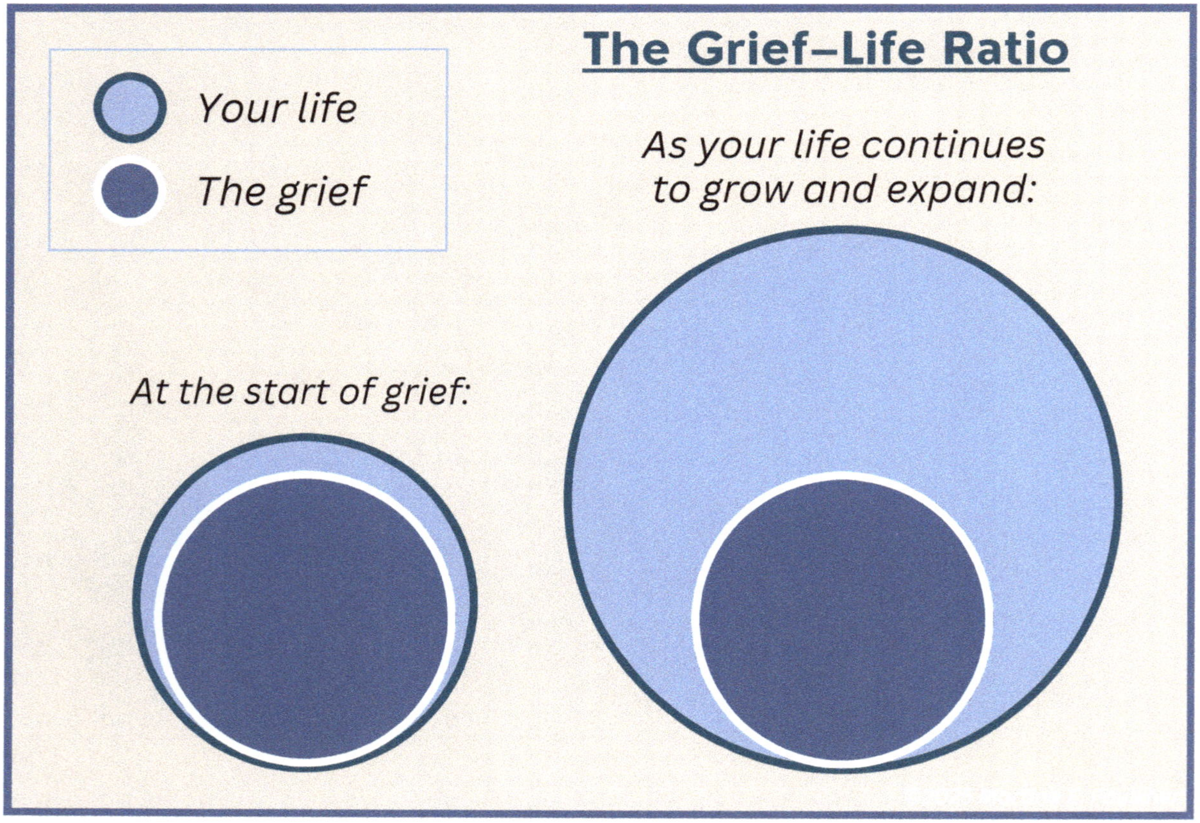

The Grief–Life Ratio

Your life

The grief

As your life continues to grow and expand:

At the start of grief:

> *"It's possible to go on, no matter how impossible it seems, and that in time, the grief… lessens. It may not go away completely, but after a while, it's not so overwhelming."*
> *— Nicholas Spark —*

The Rhythm of Grief

Does grief from death ever go away completely? Probably not, though it can. It's more often described as a cycle, actually, as if your body has some inherent intelligence about how much you can handle.

Initially, the grief may seem to come in big waves that can feel like a tsunami. You fear being drowned by them, but you somehow make it through. Then, over time, as the ratio changes, the waves also change. Though the grief does not go away completely, it can seem to get smaller as your life continues to expand.

Who Experiences Grief?

"Look closely and you will see almost everyone carrying bags of cement on their shoulders. That's why it takes courage to get out of bed in the morning and climb into the day."
— Edward Hirsch —

If you have loved someone or something, even a little, you will experience grief at some point in your life. As we have discussed, grief is inextricably tied to love. If you have loved anyone, or been invested in anything, you will grieve it when it goes. Of course, this statement assumes it will go at some point, which is true more often than not, because the one constant in life is change.

Since we can count on change, we can count on experiencing grief. Even though the depth and quality of the grief may change based on the situation, you will most likely experience it—even if it's just for a moment instead of a lifetime. Therefore, the short answer to the question is: Everyone. Everyone experiences grief at some point in their life. It is a universal emotion that is experienced very individually.

The simple reason for this is that we, as humans, are hard-wired to need connection and expression. We have a necessity to be part of something (to belong), just as we have a need to express ourselves. To avoid this basic instinct is folly and often results in regret at the end of life—and regret is a form of grief.

Other Forms of Grief

Since we know that anyone can experience grief, it stands to reason that there are other forms of grief beyond the more commonly associated expressions and experiences. These other forms of grief may not be commonly considered grief, but when we scratch beneath the surface, they are. Here are a few:

Regret is a form of grief. This is because regret is usually associated with some sense of perceived loss, such as loss of opportunity or loss of self esteem, to name two. In these examples, loss of opportunity often looks like wishing you had said something more to someone who is now gone, whereas loss of self esteem would be more like wishing you had said something different in a situation that is now passed. Regret, therefore, involves an aspect of reflection coupled with a desire for something to be different in a situation outside of your control, which is why it's a type of loss.

Furthermore, until you identify the loss behind the regret and accept that you are grieving in some way, you will find it hard to move on from the feeling. If there is loss, there is grief. And if there is grief, there needs to be mourning. This means that regret also requires some form of mourning.

Typically, when we see it in others, we meet grief with sympathy. Yet, where regret is concerned, we often treat it with disdain or dismiss it. This is also true when we are the one experiencing regret. But instead of sympathy, we should really treat regret (and grief) with empathy.

Empathy is about both allowing and understanding. When it comes to another person, it's about not trying to change their thoughts or feelings and instead focusing on doing our best to relate to what they're saying while giving them space to express.

Though we may want to change things for others to try and help ease their suffering, that's not usually helpful to the person who is suffering. Instead, we can choose to sit with them through the event and validate their feelings. This is one of the most helpful things we can offer someone who is grieving.

When it comes to ourselves, we can also use empathy to give ourselves time and space to express while simultaneously validating what it is that we are feeling, instead of trying to dismiss it or push it away out of fear or guilt. Just like all emotions tied to grief, regret needs to be expressed and processed in order to move on. In other words, when grief is involved, we need to allow ourselves and others the time and space required to mourn.

Anger can be a form of grief when it is expressed at a time of fear. When anger is about the fear of losing something, for example, it is a form of grief. For example, when a parent yells at a child for being foolish for running away from them in a parking lot, the anger is a product of the fear of potentially losing the child. The fear of loss in this case is a type of anticipatory grief expressed through anger to try and prevent it from happening again.

"Happiness is beneficial for the body, but it is grief that develops the powers of the mind."
— Marcel Proust —

Disempowerment and discouragement are forms of grief because they are often about the loss of an expected outcome. When there is an expectation with an attachment to the outcome and it doesn't come to pass, the result is often discouragement and disempowerment, both of which require a period of grieving to resolve.

Another form of disempowerment is marginalization, or being dismissed. When a person's voice (perspective, contribution, and experience) is sidelined, the resulting emotion is often one of grief expressed through sadness, frustration, and sometimes negative self-talk and hopelessness. These are all ways for the unidentified grief to manifest. Instead, it would be best to acknowledge the sense of loss, mourn it, and then refocus. Without these steps, the manifested emotions can turn into resentment, which can be harder to address.

Frustration is also a form of grief on its own. This is because it usually involves some measure of unexpressed emotion. When we cannot express ourselves fully—or are not being allowed to—the result is often a feeling of not being valid, not mattering. When we are frustrated in this way, we experience a period of loss: The loss of sense of self. In order to move through this, we need to acknowledge the loss so that we can regroup and move forward with a different plan, approach, or perspective —one that allows our voices or ideas to be expressed.

Most expressions of grief are tied to loss that has already happened. This commonality makes them a universal experience and therefore more relatable. Therefore, when thinking about who experiences grief, the answer is that we all do, or will.

Everyone experiences grief, though not everybody names it as that. Too often we focus on the symptom and not the cause. When we are feeling hopeless or discouraged, for example, we can often find loss behind the proverbial curtain. We all experience grief in different ways throughout our life and especially when we understand that grief is tied to loss—and loss is more pervasive than we may think. When we widen our definition of loss to go beyond death and life changes, we can see that it impacts more of our life than we may at first realize.

The good news is that this also means that we all understand loss and know how to deal with it. Loss is not the same across experiences, but the tools we can use to deal with it are. By shifting our perspective to be broader, we create more capacity for resilience in the face of grief. This is true for all types of grief, including a specific one that only some of us may experience.

There is a different type of grief that affects a smaller group of people. It's a type of grief that is not necessarily tied to a tangible or identifiable loss, but it is often tied to love. It's typically about something that hasn't happened yet, but that is believed (or feared) to be imminent. It's called Anticipatory Grief.

What Is Anticipatory Grief?

Briefly stated, anticipatory grief is the experience of mourning before the occurrence of a tangible or identifiable loss. When we know loss is going to happen, but we don't know when, we move into a space of anticipatory grief. This is most commonly experienced with chronic and terminal illness, both on the part of the patient as well as on those who will be left behind, such as family, friends, and caretakers.

Anticipatory grief is sometimes harder to navigate because it is compounded by other emotions, such as guilt, fear, confusion, sadness, and aggravation or exhaustion, to name a few. The biggest of these emotions is often guilt.

A pervasive sense of guilt can often accompany anticipatory grief, predominantly because we don't understand why (or accept) we are grieving. The person is still with us, so it seems illogical to be experiencing grief. That thought then carries over to feelings of selfishness which can lead to guilt.

But the truth is that in anticipatory grief there are two layers of grief occurring at the same time:

- Grief at the actual loss of "normal" we once shared and enjoyed with the person

- Grief at the anticipated loss of their presence in the future

Even though someone is still alive, they may not still be alive in the same way that they once were if they are experiencing decline. This means that we are grieving the loss of opportunity to spend time with them in the way we always had. We've lost our sense of "normal". Additionally, as it becomes clear that there is an end on the horizon, we begin to anticipate the tangible loss of the person. Thus, we start to grieve, even if we don't name it that.

Change in this way invites grief into your life in ways nothing else can. Even though we may know that our elders will one day be gone, there is no way for us to pre-plan our grief. Even the most mentally healthy among us will experience grief in ways they never could have anticipated once the event happens. This is why you can't plan for grief, including anticipatory grief.

"Anything that's human is mentionable, and anything that is mentionable, can be more manageable. When we can talk about our feelings, they become less overwhelming, less upsetting, and less scary. The people we trust with that important talk can help us know that we are not alone."

— Fred Rogers —

The best way to deal with anticipatory grief is to identify the two aspects that are influencing your emotions, and then allowing yourself to process them and mourn.

- It is okay to mourn the loss of somebody before they're physically gone from your life, in fact, it's important that you do. When you identify that you are mourning the loss of how things used to be, you are better able to show up with empathy and kindness for yourself and them.

- It is also okay to mourn the projections you are experiencing when you think about a future without them in your life. By acknowledging that you will be affected by this loss, it can help to make you more focused on the present, enjoying their company now.

Regardless of whether it's traditional grief or anticipatory grief, the underlying truth remains the same: Grief is highly individual and personal. Since we will all experience grief at some point in our lives, often multiple times, we must accept this truth in order to be flexible and move with it. This means that everyone experiences grief and there is no one way to express or deal with it.

How Do We Express Grief?

"But there was no need to be ashamed of tears, for tears bore witness that a man had the greatest of courage, the courage to suffer."

— Viktor E. Frankl —

Depending on your culture and environment, your expression of grief may vary. This is to say that different people, communities, and societies express grief in different ways, and none are better or worse than the other. As such, we can instead look at where we express grief in our bodies, which can transcend any society, practice, or culture.

Grief is most commonly expressed through tears. When we are overcome by grief and sadness, we cry. It is suggested that when we release tears, our body receives this as a signal to also release feel-good chemicals, like endorphins and oxytocin.

These feel-good chemicals help to regulate our system as we move through the phases of grief. They also serve to help us physically, because when we are in grief, we can actually hurt or feel pain in our bodies.

Historically, grief is related to statements like, "broken-hearted" or "my heart hurts". This is because we are sensory beings.

One of the ways we are able to make sense of the world is through our interactions with it on a physical level, which includes our five senses. As sensory beings, it stands to reason that we need to process our emotions physically as well as mentally and emotionally.

This means that regardless of the type of grief we are experiencing (physical, emotional, or both), we need to use our physical being to help us process the loss because that's how we're made.

The pain we feel physically is a signal to our brains that it's time to do something physical to help process the overwhelming emotion. Sometimes, we do this through physical activity, such as running, cleaning, or sobbing. But we also do it through less-healthy endeavors such as over-eating or starving ourselves, sex, and engaging in numbing activities, like gaming or binge-watching media. When we don't process our grief (or other emotions), it can show up dysfunctionally, such as when we lash out at others.

Our Five Senses

Hearing
Sight • Smell
Taste • Touch

The bottom line is that if we don't actively work to identify, acknowledge, and process our grief, it will still find a way to be expressed and it will come out of us, often sideways. This is what can ultimately damage relationships the most, leading to more potential loss. And more grief.

Expressing grief in healthy ways—through physical, mental, and emotional means—is the best way to give yourself the help you need to heal. How you choose to grieve is up to you; nobody can do it for you, nor choose for you. The most important thing you can do is allow yourself to grieve. Give yourself permission to take the time and space you need to listen to your heart, feel the grief, and express it.

Unfortunately, sometimes there is a stigma around expressing grief, such as when someone thinks your grief "should be over" because "enough time has passed." Even if these statements are made with the best of intentions (wanting you to feel better), as a society, we would do well to normalize grief as part of life. When we understand that it is, we become more accepting of others' journeys through grief, which may, in turn, help them move through the most intense aspects of grieving with more grace.

> *"When you are sorrowful look again in your heart, and you shall see that in truth you are weeping for that which has been your delight."*
>
> — Kahlil Gibran —

At the end of the day, feeling grief in your body is normal and it requires a tangible approach to healing. A healthy intervention can include movement, counseling, journaling, and practicing self-care.

The first step is to understand that you are a sensory being, which means that you have the capacity to feel grief in multiple ways and probably will. By accepting this, you become better able to manage and move through grief.

The second step is to find outlets for your grief—whether they are group-related or individual outlets does not matter. What you want to focus on is finding things that support you in your grieving process, whatever that looks like for you.

Why Do We Grieve?

We grieve because our minds and bodies need to express the emotion behind loss. That is the simplest answer, but it's actually more than that. The bigger picture includes an aspect of needing to make sense of something that we possibly don't want to—or aren't ready and willing to—accept.

The grieving period gives us time to shift from denial to acceptance.

Grief is a common experience. We all understand it, even if we understand it differently in its nuances and expressions. Sometimes, we can know when someone else is experiencing grief just by looking at them. This is because we know grief, as individuals and as a species. We also know grief enough to apply it to other species as well.

Wildlife researchers have identified elephant grieving behaviors such as: holding vigil, touching, making noise, and showing reverence. When we watch elephants in videos, we can relate to their grief at the loss of a member of the pack. Or when we see dogs lie on their owner's grave, we know this is a sign of grieving. We may be anthropomorphizing the animal, but we do so because we know grief when we see it, even across species.

So, why do we grieve? What purpose does grief serve? By now, you know that grief serves to bring us to acceptance by bridging the gap from one reality to a new reality. It also helps us process emotions to help ourselves heal, especially when it prompts our brain to release feel-good chemicals. This is survival at its best. Our brain wants to keep us alive and may see an overflow of emotions as a potential threat to our survival, so it fixes it by releasing chemicals to help. There is, however, more to discuss when it comes to grief, including the two extremes at either end of the spectrum of grief:

- Grief and depression
- Grief avoidance or not feeling the need to grieve

Grief and Depression

Everyone handles loss differently. We know this to be true. For some, the experience of grief can lead to something more seemingly permanent: depression. In truth, there are specific clinical measurements that a trained mental health professional must use to properly diagnose depression, especially Major Depressive Disorder (MDD). A clinical diagnosis of major depression is different from a person who is cycling through grief in ways that keep them stuck in the cycle. In both cases, working with a professional is important.

Where grief is concerned, it is important to note that grief does not automatically lead to depression, though they can share symptoms or look similar. To understand this better, it's important to note that grief can typically be tied to loss of some kind, whereas depression does not need a loss correlation.

So, what is going on when a person is grieving seemingly endlessly in ways that mimic a major depressive episode? Is it self-indulgent, or is it the body's way of trying to process something it just can't understand? Let's return to an earlier statement: The grieving period gives us time to shift from denial to acceptance.

If the loss is never accepted, the grief can cycle endlessly and lead the person to a form of persistent depression. For this, they will need more help from professionals, possibly including medication. Medicinal treatment for mental health is often stigmatized, but it shouldn't be. The body is made up of chemicals, and if some of those chemicals are over-firing or not firing at all, the body may need medicinal support to rebalance.

When a person is chronically cycling through grief in ways that share symptoms with depression (or, in fact, if the grief triggers depression), then medicinal support is not only warranted, it could be life-changing.

At the other end of the spectrum, there are some individuals who may not feel the need to grieve, even though they have experienced loss. Though this may seem uncommon, it may not be as rare as you think. Why does this matter? Because just as we need to normalize expressions of grief, we also need to accept and normalize that not everybody feels the need to grieve, whether it's right now, or ever.

What if I Don't Feel the Need to Grieve?

As we know, there is no singular-prescribed period for grief. Grief is highly individual. However, if a person seems to be stuck in the cycle of grief, it may be time to intervene in other ways to help give them the support they need to come to a place of acceptance. Even though grief may never fully leave us, the quality of the grief can change over time, and typically does unless it's become cyclical, continually reinforcing itself.

Remember, grief is entirely individual even though it's a universal experience. There is nothing "wrong" with someone who does not feel the need to grieve. Just as there is nothing wrong with someone who feels the need to grieve. Unfortunately, we often project our own expectations and understanding of grief on others, which can lead to experiences of shame or guilt for not grieving or for grieving too much or in the wrong ways.

If someone does not feel the need to grieve a loss, the best thing to do is to support them in this decision. There may be many reasons why this is their experience or choice, such as:

- They are in denial, and need to remain there for the foreseeable future to protect their mental health. This could mean that they will grieve eventually,

once they have more mental and emotional space, or it could mean that they never grieve this particular loss.

- The nature of their relationship to the loss is not what it appeared to be. This is particularly apt when we hear someone speaking ill of a person who has died, or simply not grieving. If a death brings a sense of freedom to the person who is left behind, then it's likely that others have made assumptions about their relationship.

- They process grief differently. This is more common across cultural divides, but not solely socially different. There are people who have done so much self-work that they process grief very quickly and internally, which can look like they are not grieving to others. They may be grieving, or they may not be grieving. Either way, it's entirely personal.

Of course, there are many more reasons why someone may not feel the need to grieve. What matters is that we are accepting of the individual choice to grieve and we provide support and understanding along the way. Someone who does not feel the need to grieve now may suddenly be blind-sided by grief at a distant point in the future. They will need support and understanding. Similarly, someone who is stuck in a cycle of grief also needs support and understanding.

When we understand that we grieve to make sense of something that is outside of our control, to bring us from denial to acceptance, we are better able to not only process our own grief but also be supportive of others who are grieving.

How Can I Heal From Grief?

"You will survive, and you will find purpose in the chaos. Moving on doesn't mean letting go."

— Mary VanHaute —

Healing from grief is a process. There is no magic wand, no specific timeline, and no pill or prescription you can take to "fix" your grief. The good news is that there is one certainty about grief: If you allow yourself to move through it and with it, it changes.

The quality and quantity of the grief you experience changes. Over time, though you may still be able to tap into the original sensation of grief, and you may be able to identify and feel the loss on a regular basis, it still changes. It becomes less intense when you allow yourself to process it and flow with it.

Conversely, when you try to tamp it down, stuff it away, or make it rigid by trying to fit it into a specific box or framework, it can become more consuming, more fixed in your being. This is often what happens when you see someone constantly cycling through grief.

Healing from grief, like all emotions, needs you to be willing. It requires your active participation as well as your flexibility. In order to heal from grief, you need to both address it and not focus on it.

In other words, you need to identify it, work with it when it arises, and when it fades from view for a little while, you need to allow it to do so. By engaging in this dance with your focus, you begin to heal.

Unfortunately, we can feel guilty when we suddenly realize we are laughing, even though we are in the midst of grief having lost someone. The remedy for the guilt is to put our attention back on the loss. Sometimes this is a good idea, and sometimes it's not.

By allowing ourselves to flow with the emotions that arise, we give ourselves permission to continue to participate in life, even when we are in the midst of grief. As a result, we become more resilient, more empathic, and more understanding of ourselves and others.

This, ultimately, is what leads to healing from grief... and almost anything. The goal is not to live without grief; the goal is to understand that it's okay to live with grief. To keep living. To experience life, even in the face of loss, and enjoy it.

More Notes On Grief

"There is no grief like the grief that does not speak."

— Henry Wadsworth —

Grief is universal, and when it's universally understood, we need to be cautious about taking on someone else's grief. As kind and thoughtful humans, when we see someone in pain, we can have a tendency to want to "fix" it. Though this may feel like a thoughtful gesture, unless you are a doctor in an emergency room, it's not actually helpful in the long run.

Taking on someone else's grief looks like doing things for them so that they don't feel the emotional waves. In other words, you try to redirect the tsunami, often toward yourself. However, when you do this, you are denying them the opportunity to grow. You are taking away their chance to improve their resilience and become happier in their life. It may seem counterintuitive, but it's true.

Allowing someone to experience their grief is not only necessary, it's imperative for their growth—mentally, emotionally, and even physically. By experiencing grief and learning how to navigate it, they are creating tools that they can use in the future to create a healthier and better life.

So, what can you do when you see someone hurting from grief? Instead of doing things for them, you do things with them. You can sit with them. You can draw on your own experience of empathy and show compassion and understanding. If needed, you can provide resources as suggestions, not tasks to complete. In short, you can be with them—which may be more valuable than anything else you can provide.

> "Everyone must leave something behind when he dies, my grandfather said. A child or a book or a painting or a house or a wall built or a pair of shoes made. Or a garden planted.
>
> Something your hand touches some way so your soul has somewhere to go when you die, and when people look at that tree or that flower you planted, you're there."
>
> — Ray Bradbury, Fahrenheit 451 —

Resources For Grief

"Your grief path is yours alone, and no one else can walk it, and no one else can understand it."

— Terri Irwin —

Though there are many resources available to people experiencing grief, there are two that stand above the rest: Process/Grief Groups and Journaling. This is because one helps you to connect with others so that you feel less alone in your journey and the other helps you to connect with yourself so that you can begin to make sense of your feelings on the journey. Both can be incredibly helpful to anyone experiencing grief.

Process Groups—Attending a grief process group helps in multiple ways, but perhaps the most important is that it helps to normalize the experience, helping the person to feel less alone in their grief. Our human nature is hard-wired for connection; we crave belonging.

When we undergo something that changes our world and our life in significant ways, it is incredibly helpful to feel like we are still part of something.

The grief group provides a safe space to share feelings, fears, and thoughts regarding this significant change. It also gives language to the experience that we might not otherwise have.

Being able to speak to the grief with words that help it all make sense is incredibly important, especially in being able to express needs and expectations to others in our life.

Journaling—Whether it's free-form or prompted, journaling is something that can really help us make sense of our thoughts and feelings. It allows us to process what's going on in our heads and our bodies in a safe way, in our own time, and at a pace that we need. It's also incredibly flexible.

You can journal anywhere at any time. There is no limit to how, when, or where you can write. There are also multiple ways you can journal, from using actual pen and paper, to creating a digital journal on your devices. The only caution would be ensuring that both a paper and a digital journal are protected.

Once you have done this, journaling is a highly effective way to navigate the ups and downs of grief, helping you to make sense of the situation and move from denial to acceptance.

Regardless of whether you are moving through grief yourself or helping someone else, the most important thing to remember is that it is a highly individual experience.

Keeping this simple truth in mind will allow you to have more grace in both situations, which is good for everyone.

Conclusion

Understanding grief is about understanding that all humans are unique while also being similar. Grief is one of the most universally-experienced emotions, and yet, it can be expressed in almost as many ways as there are people on the planet. Where there is overlap, we find aspects of community, religion, society, and tradition. But the actual internalized experience will always be unique to the individual.

More often than not, to be in grief is to have loved. To experience grief is to know loss. To move through grief is to grow. Through grief, we build resilience, compassion, and understanding. Through grief, we honor the love we are capable of feeling for someone or something. Through grief, we gain a deeper sense of what we value and hold dear.

If you don't know if you're experiencing grief, but you feel out of sorts from a situation, ask yourself if you are experiencing loss. Since loss can take many forms, including things we may not normally think of, being able to identify it is key to healing. Once you've identified something as loss, you can now allow yourself the time you need to mourn, so that you can heal.

It is nearly impossible to live a life in which you don't grieve. In this way, grief, above all else, is both the price we pay for being human, as well as one of life's greatest gifts. Because a life without grief potentially also means a life without love, without investment, without passion, joy, and hope. Grief reminds us that we are alive, that we are all connected, and that we have loved and can love. It helps us remember that we can invest in people and experiences that bring us joy, even though we know we can also lose them.

Grief, therefore, is the ultimate teacher of what it means to be human. When we can move through grief and get to a place where we understand it and learn how to live with it, we suddenly realize what it means to truly live and our life is all the better for it.

> *"The quality of your life is based on the choices you make."*
> — Martina E. Faulkner —

About the Author

Martina E. Faulkner is a cross-genre author whose work focuses primarily on exploring what it means to be human, both the unique and the universal. She holds a trifecta in the mental health/healing world as a therapist, certified life coach, and Reiki Master Teacher. This distinctive background allows her to draw on her professional and personal experience in her writing, whether fiction, nonfiction, or poetry.

A self-proclaimed Anglophile, Martina drinks tea daily, loves walks in nature, and enjoys looking at beautiful images from the British Isles while dreaming up her next book. You can read her regular column ('Unique and Universal') on Substack, follow her on Instagram and Facebook @martinaefaulkner, or visit martinaefaulkner.com.

As a children's author Martina's debut children's book, <u>When the World Went Quiet</u>, was given as a gift to Sir David Attenborough, who referred to it as "charming."

Other Books

Understanding Karma
50 and F*ck It!
What if..?
Love and Pain
Infinite In My Heart
Me: 365
The Author's Journey
Crafting the Perfect College Essay

Children's Books

When the World Went Quiet
Princess Wigglebottom and the Forgotten Christmas